+ Anima Vol.3

Created By Natsumi Mukai

Translation - Alethea and Athena Nibley
English Adaption - Karen Ahlstrom
Copy Editor - Stephanie Duchin
Layout and Lettering - Star Print Brokers
Cover Layout - James Lee

Editor - Troy Lewter
Digital Imaging Manager - Chris Buford
Pre-Press Supervisor - Erika Terriquez
Art Director - Anne-Marie Horne
Managing Editor - Vy Nguyen
Production Manager - Elisabeth Brizzi
VP of Production - Ron Klamert
Editor-in-Chief - Rob Tokar
Publisher - Mike Kiley
President and C.O.O. - John Parker
C.E.O. and Chief Creative Officer - Stuart Levy

A  Manga

TOKYOPOP Inc.
5900 Wilshire Blvd. Suite 2000
Los Angeles, CA 90036

E-mail: info@TOKYOPOP.com
Come visit us online at www.TOKYOPOP.com

ISBN: 978-1-4278-0443-3

First TOKYOPOP printing: February 2007

10 9 8 7 6 5 4 3 2 1

Printed in the USA

Volume 3
by Natsumi Mukai

HAMBURG // LONDON // LOS ANGELES // TOKYO

+ A N I M A

迎夏生
NATSUMI MUKAI

STORY & CHARACTERS

The +Anima are beings that possess animal-like powers. Cooro, a crow +Anima, peeks in at a circus during his travels and meets Husky, a fish +Anima who is playing a mermaid princess in the show. Though Cooro invites Husky to run away from the circus and join him on his travels, he refuses. Husky is tired of the circus life, though, and waiting for the ringmaster to fall asleep, he plans to leave Cooro and run away himself. However, the ringmaster is one step ahead of them. He captures Husky and forces him to continue playing the mermaid princess, with Cooro added to the show as the angel of death. Thanks to Cooro's quick thinking, the two soon get their chance to escape. Though circus people surround them, Cooro uses his +Anima power to carry Husky into the sky, and the two leave the circus far behind them.

クーロ [Cooro]

**Crow +Anima.
When he spreads his pitch-black wings, he can fly freely in the sky.
He is a bit of a glutton!**

ハスキー [Husky]

**Fish +Anima. He can swim freely through water like a merman.
He's a little stubborn, and he hates girls.**

NO WAY! I'M NOT FLYING WITH YOU AGAIN!!
HUH?

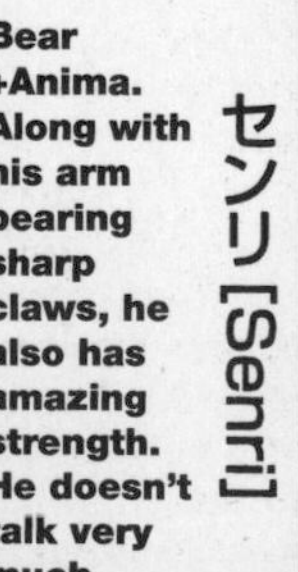

センリ [Senri]

Bear +Anima. Along with his arm bearing sharp claws, he also has amazing strength. He doesn't talk very much.

**At the village of Abon, the two of them meet Senri, a bear +Anima who was protecting a field of special plants.
The three chase off The Garrison Gang, local thugs who thought there was a gold mine under the field. As peace returns to the village, Senri's duties as a bodyguard have come to an end, so he joins Cooro and Husky as they travel onward.**

ナナ [Nana]

Bat +Anima. She can fly and use an ultrasonic screech. A fashion-conscious girl, she is scared of forests at night.

In the underground ruins beneath the metropolis Octopus, Husky's pearls are stolen, and Cooro and the others meet the bat +Anima, Nana. They soon solve the crime and move on. Nana wants to travel with the party, but Husky, who hates girls for some reason, refuses to let Nana join them, and leaves the party himself. Nana goes after Husky, and tells him the story of how she was awakened as a +Anima, and he finally accepts her as one of the group.
And thus the journey begins...

ローズ [Rose]

Cat +Anima. A girl Cooro and the others met on their journey. She works by herself to make and sell accessories. She has a little brother who is almost eight years old.

イグナス [Igneous]

フライ [Fly]

During their travels, the party meets the peddler Rose, and crosses the mountain pass with her. It seems the journey will go smoothly, but then they encounter Igneous, a commander of the Astarian Military. Igneous hates the mountain people Kim-un-kur (Senri's clan), and the narrow mountain pathway is thrown into confusion. Working together with Rose, Cooro and the others manage to settle things and arrive in town. The party says goodbye to Rose and continues its journey.
And who is the mysterious Researcher who seems to knows an awful lot about Cooro? What awaits the four young +Anima at the end of their journey?

CONTENTS

Chapter 9
Wings of the Wind—Part 1 09

Chapter 10
Wings of the Wind—Part 2 41

Chapter 11
Guardian Heart—Part 1 73

Chapter 12
Guardian Heart—Part 2 105

Chapter 13
Husky's Melancholy...136

Chapter 14
Scars 169

Chapter 9:
Wings of the Wind — Part 1

HUSKY, WE DID IT!
JUST TWO MORE, OKAY?
EASY FOR YOU TO SAY! WHY DON'T YOU DO A BETTER JOB OF HERDING THEM OVER HERE!
COORO, HUSKY... GOOD LUCK!

HUH...?

OH!
THERE'S SOME!

!

EH?!
Hey!

COORO!!
HEY! WHERE ARE YOU GOING?!
...

IT IS A PERSON!
OR... IS IT... A BIRD +ANIMA...?
HUH?

OOOF!!
AAAW!

NO...
OH, MAN...!
H-HEY...! HANG IN THERE!
I HAVEN'T SEEN HIM BEFORE...
?
WAIT... WHERE DID THESE FEATHERS COME FROM...?
UNNNGH...
SAY... ARE YOU ALL RIGHT?

...?
I... WHAT HAPPENED ...?
MY GLIDER FELL AND CRASHED INTO YOU.
SORRY ABOUT THAT.

AW, NO WORRIES! IT HURTS A LITTLE, BUT I'M FINE!

WHEW! THAT'S A RELIEF!

WELL, THEN...
OH! ALLOW ME TO HELP!
HUH?
R-REALLY?

I'M COORO!

NICE TO MEET 'CHA, COORO. I'M SHADOW.

HEY THERE, SHADOW...

Heh heh!

LOOKS LIKE YOU FAILED AGAIN, HUH?

SHUT UP! THE WIND WAS BAD TODAY, THAT'S ALL!

I'LL SHOW YOU SOON ENOUGH...

DANGIT ...!

IS THAT YOUR HOUSE, SHADOW?

NAH. IT'S MORE MY SHED THAN MY HOUSE.

MY REAL HOUSE IS ON TOP OF THAT MOUNTAIN.

REALLY?

OH!

I **KNEW** IT! EVEN THE **REEL** IS **BROKEN**!

Dangit!!!

REEL...? WHAT IS IT FOR?

YOU... REALLY WANT TO KNOW?
YEAH!
WELL, YOU WEAR THE GLIDER ON YOUR BACK, AND THE REEL FEEDS OUT THE LINE...
FWIP
...AND YOU LAUNCH FROM THE TOP OF THAT HILL.
IF I CAN MANAGE TO RIDE ON THE WIND CURRENTS IN THESE PASSES...
...I SHOULD BE ABLE TO *FLY* OVER THE *MOUNTAINS!*
OH ...

WOW, SHADOW!
THAT'S GREAT!
ぴょん
ぴょん
Y-YEAH...?
YOU REALLY THINK SO? SO YOU UNDERSTAND, COORO? COOL!

THE ONLY THING IS...
...WITHOUT AN ASSISTANT, I JUST CAN'T GET IT TO WORK.
SO, I WAS THINKING... WILL YOU HELP ME?

I'LL GIVE YOU SOME YUMMY CHEESE FOR YOUR TROUBLE...!
CHEESE?!
キラーー

OKAY! I'LL DO IT, I'LL DO IT!!
ALL RIGHT, THEN! LET'S EAT!

I WONDER HOW FAR COORO WENT.
HE'S TAKING A REALLY LONG TIME COMING BACK...
FORGET ABOUT HIM. HE'S SUCH A CHILD!
CHILD? BUT HUSKY, AREN'T YOU A CHILD, TOO?
NOT THE POINT! I'M *SAYING* HE'S *LIKE* A THREE-YEAR-OLD!
HE'D GET LOST CHASING A BUTTERFLY...
...AND THEN HE WOULDN'T EVEN REALIZE HE'S LOST.
BUTTER-FLY!
HE'S PROBABLY FORGOTTEN ALL ABOUT US!

......

?
......
?

COORO.

WELL, IT IS COORO.
HE'LL COME BACK WHEN HE GETS HUNGRY!

IT'S GOOD, ISN'T IT? MY DAD MAKES IT AT THE FARM ON TOP OF THE MOUNTAIN.
IT'S GOAT CHEESE.

ABOUT THIS GLIDER...

WHERE WILL YOU GO IN IT?

WELL, UNTIL A YEAR AGO...
...I HERDED GOATS WITH MY FAMILY ON TOP OF THE MOUNTAIN.
THERE'S ONLY ONE NARROW PATH DOWN TO THIS VILLAGE AT THE FOOT OF THE MOUNTAIN.
AND IT... COLLAPSED IN A STORM...
AT THE SAME TIME, ELENA CAME DOWN WITH A FEVER...
IF ONLY SHE HAD MEDICINE, SHE WOULD HAVE BEEN OKAY...!

YOU MEAN... SHE DIED...?
UM...
sniffle
Y-YEAH.
TH-THAT'S WHY...
...I HAVE TO MAKE THE GLIDER WORK. SO I CAN GET MEDICINE TO THE TOP OF THE MOUNTAIN WHEN IT'S NEEDED!
I WANT TO RIDE ON THE WIND...
...JUST LIKE A BIRD!
AT FIRST, I ONLY CARED ABOUT GETTING THE GLIDER TO FLY...
...BUT... GRADUALLY, I STARTED WANTING TO FLY MYSELF.
HOW GREAT WOULD IT BE IF I COULD FLY LIKE A BIRD TO THE TOP OF THE MOUNTAIN!

YEAH!
IT DOES FEEL GREAT!
HUH?
WE'RE GOING TO FIX THIS, RIGHT?
ER... YEAH.
R-RIGHT! WE'LL FIX IT TONIGHT AND TRY AGAIN!
YEAH!

ヒュオオオ…
ザワザワ
SPLISH
SPLISH
COORO... HE NEVER CAME BACK...
LOOKS LIKE A STORM'S COMING.
THAT IDIOT...!
WHERE DID HE GO...?

ヒョオオ
HEY, SHADOW...
ARE YOU REALLY PLANNING TO FLY IN WIND LIKE THIS?
YOU BET!

IF IT CAN'T FLY DURING A STORM, IT'S NO USE TO ME.
THIS IS A GOOD CHANCE TO TEST ITS LIMITS!

BUT ON A DAY LIKE THIS, THE AIR IS HEAVY, WHICH MEANS IT'S HARD TO CATCH THE WIND...WHICH IN TURN MEANS IT'S ALSO HARD TO FLY.
SO BE CAREFUL, OKAY?

HUH...? UH-HUH, SURE...
ALL RIGHT THEN, COORO--MAN THE REEL!
たたた
OKAY!

I WONDER IF IT WOULD BE EASIER TO FLY WITHOUT THIS ROPE...
OKAY! HERE I GO!

HAH!
W-WITHOUT WIND LIKE THIS...
...I CAN'T GO TO THE TOP OF THE MOUNTAIN!!
!!
OOF!!

WAAAAAHH!!
SHADOW!!

GWAAAHH!!
HUNNH!!

WHOA!!

WH-WHAT JUST HAPPENED...?

ANOTHER FEATHER...

SHADOW!!

ARE YOU OKAY?!

C-COORO...?!
Y-YOU HAVE WINGS...?!

EH...?
OH...! WELL, I'M A +ANIMA.
+ANIMA...?

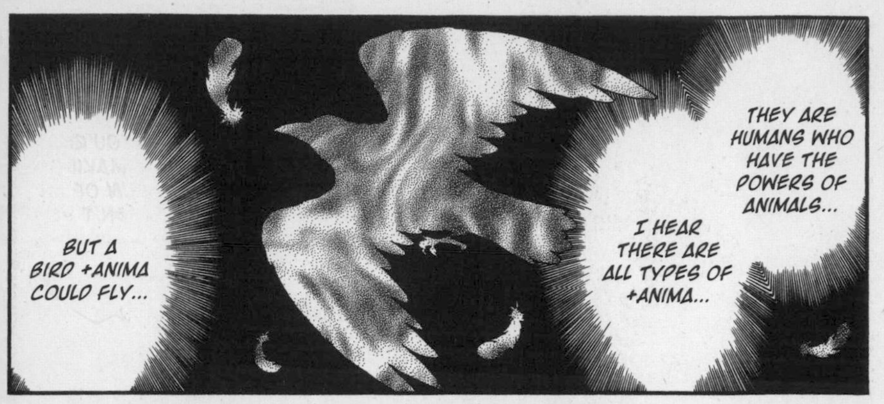
THEY ARE HUMANS WHO HAVE THE POWERS OF ANIMALS...
I HEAR THERE ARE ALL TYPES OF +ANIMA...
BUT A BIRD +ANIMA COULD FLY...

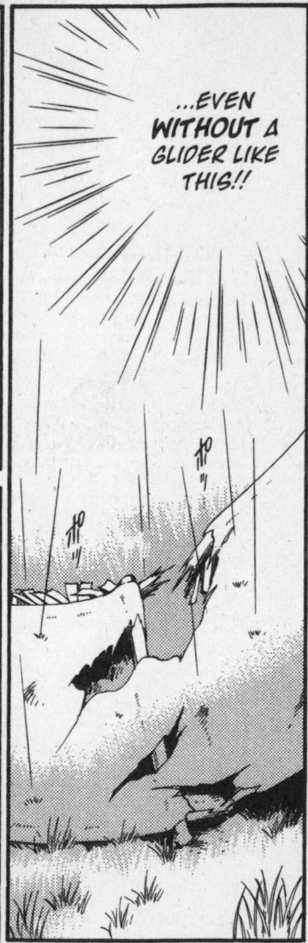
...EVEN WITHOUT A GLIDER LIKE THIS!!

AW... IT BROKE AGAIN...
BUT DON'T WORRY-- I'LL HELP YOU FIX IT!

COORO ...
YES, SHADOW?

YOU'RE... MAKING ***FUN*** OF ME, AREN'T YOU?

YOU HAD WINGS THIS WHOLE TIME...

YOU MUST THINK IT'S HILARIOUS THAT I'M STRUGGLING WITH THESE FAKE ONES!

J-JUST
GO
AWAY!
FLAP THOSE
WINGS OF
YOURS AWAY
FROM HERE!!

ザアアア
ガラ
ガラ

THE RAIN'S GOTTEN REALLY BAD...
I'VE GOT A BAD FEELING ABOUT THIS...

THERE WAS A STORM LIKE THIS ON THAT DAY, AS WELL...
ELENA ...

ドンドンドン

SHADOW!

H-HURRY TO THE DOCTOR'S HOUSE!

WHAT? WHAT'S WRONG?!

YOUR DAD'S THERE...! COME ON!

HE SAYS ***FEVER'S*** BROKEN OUT ON THE ***MOUNTAIN FARM*** AGAIN!

!

He is downhearted with shock.

DAD!!

WHAT'S THIS ABOUT A FEVER?!

AH! SHADOW!

S-SO WHO'S SICK?!

IT GOT DONNA... CAROL AND MOLLY...

SO LET'S GET THE MEDICINE TO THEM!

I CAME DOWN THE MOUNTAIN TO GET IT, BUT...
...ON MY WAY, THE ROAD COLLAPSED!
NO...

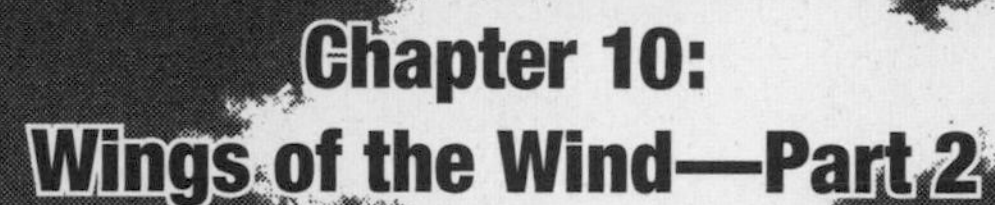

Chapter 10: Wings of the Wind—Part 2

ゴボ…
THE WATER...
ゴボッ
THE WATER'S SO HEAVY...
ゴボボボッ
I CAN'T BREATHE...
I...
I DON'T WANT TO DIE...!!
ハッ

PWUH?!
ゴボッ
GASP! WHAT'S WITH THIS WATER?!
S-SENRI! NANA?!
ザバッ
WE WERE SUPPOSED TO BE NAPPING TOGETHER ...
AH! HUSKY! YOU'RE AWAKE?
HUH?!
WHAT THE--?! WHY DIDN'T YOU TWO WAKE ME UP?!

THE POND FLOODED BECAUSE OF THE RAIN...
...BUT WE THOUGHT SINCE YOU'RE PART FISH, YOU'D BE FINE.
チャプ
チャプ
THAT'S NOT THE PROBLEM!!

SENRI! DON'T JUST **SIT THERE!** HELP ME EXPLAIN IT TO HER!!

FLAP
FLAP FLAP
!

COORO ...?!
WHAT...?
I HEARD WINGS!

AH! OVER THERE!

WAIT...!

COOORO!!

IT'S NO USE...
SHADOW, THERE'S NO WAY WE CAN GET TO THE MOUNTAIN FARM!

NO...!

SHADOW?!

SHADOW! DON'T TELL ME...
...YOU'RE PLANNING TO FLY THIS WORN-OUT OLD GLIDER?!
DON'T! YOU'LL DIE!!

IF I DON'T USE IT *NOW*...
...THEN WHAT WAS THE POINT OF *MAKING IT* IN THE *FIRST PLACE?!*

LOOK!
HE'S OVER THERE!
COORO!
WHERE WERE YOU?!
WE ATE ALL THE FISH, YOU KNOW!

?
COORO? WHAT IS IT? WHAT'S WRONG?
DOES YOUR TUMMY HURT?

UH-UH...

OH!!
ばっ
SNIFF...

SENRI...?

HURT.

WHAT? YOU'RE HURT?!

UH-UH. IT DOESN'T HURT ANYMORE...
I'M JUST... KIND OF... TIRED...
COORO?

I WANTED TO STAY WITH HIM LONGER... BUT HE TOLD ME TO GO AWAY.
WE WERE GETTING ALONG SO WELL...
HE EVEN GAVE ME CHEESE.

CHEESE?!
...
THAT'S IT! WHERE WERE YOU?!
THE VILLAGE OVER THERE.

A VILLAGE?! YOU SHOULD HAVE SAID SO SOONER!
HUH?
WE CAN GO THERE TO GET OUT OF THE RAIN! HURRY!

HMM... I WONDER WHAT'S GOING ON...?

SHADOW! DON'T!!
IT'S CRAZY!!
SHADOW!
WHAT IS THAT FLYING THING?!
WHAT'S WRONG WITH SHADOW?!
COME BACK!!
HEEEEYY!!

HE SAID HE'S GOING TO TAKE MEDICINE TO THE MOUNTAIN FARM.
THE PATH IS COLLAPSED, SO WE CAN'T USE IT!
That's no reason to go up in that crazy contraption!
SHADOW ...

......

COORO...

IS HE THE ONE WHO TOLD YOU TO GO AWAY?

EH?

OH... YEAH.

THAT'S JUST SO TYPICAL OF YOU, COORO!
YOU REALLY SHOULDN'T LISTEN TO EVERYTHING ANYONE TELLS YOU!
IF YOU WANT TO GO, YOU SHOULD JUST FLY UP THERE!
HUSKY...
ポカン…
HE CHASED YOU AWAY, BUT YOU STILL DON'T HATE HIM, RIGHT?
YEAH...
THEN GO, ALREADY!
ドンッ
AH!
YEAH... I WILL!

SIGH...
HE NEEDS SO MUCH HELP.
YEP.

AND *YOU'RE* THE BEST ONE TO HELP HIM, AREN'T YOU, HUSKY?
WHAT?!

HURK...!

GRRAAHHHH!!

WAAH!!

NOT ONLY IS THE AIR HEAVY, BUT I CAN'T READ THE WIND!
IT'S THROWING ME AROUND SO MUCH, I CAN'T EVEN GO UP THE MOUNTAIN!!

COOORO!!

SHIFT YOUR WEIGHT TO THE LEFT!
WAAAH!!
SHADOW!
YOU CAN RIDE THIS WIND!
AH...
AH... AH... AH!

LET GO!!
I SAID GO AWAY-- SO GO AWAY!!
JUST LEAVE ME ALONE!!

I...
...DON'T HAVE THE RIGHT... TO ASK YOU TO DO THIS!
SO JUST GO AWAY!
NOPE!!

ALL RIGHT! HERE COMES THE NEXT WIND!
WAAAHH!!

ザー……
ヒュウウー…
WHAT IN THE...?
ザザザァアッ
OOOOHH!!

MOM! I HAVE MEDICINE!
HOW ARE DONNA AND THE OTHERS?!
SHADOOW!!
THEY'LL BE JUST FINE...
...NOW THAT WE HAVE MEDICINE! WE CAN TAKE CARE OF A LITTLE FEVER THANKS TO YOU!
Everyone! Shadow brought medicine!
Yay!
Now we'll be okay!
WHEW...
THANK GOODNESS ...!
COORO ...
THANK Y--
OH!
Zzzzz...

THANK YOU...
... COORO.

NNH...
Baaaaa!
Baaaaaaaa!
FWIP
Baaaaaa!
Baa!
Baa!
タッ

COORO!
DID THE FEVER GO AWAY?
IT DID, RIGHT?!
WAAH!
ぐいぐい

THIS IS DONNA, CAROL AND MOLLY.
THEY'RE GOATS...
Baaaa!
Baaaa!

NOT JUST GOATS... THEY'RE ALL LIKE MY DEAR LITTLE SISTERS.
OH...
I'M GLAD!

OH YEAH...!

WE HAVE MORE OF THEIR CHEESE UP HERE.

HAVE SOME!

CHEESE!!

CHEESE! CHEESE!!
IT'S REALLY GOOD, YES?

Meanwhile, at the collapsed mountain road...
DARN THAT COORO...!
HE'S NOT COMING BACK!

UMPH?

Antimonopoly !

Chapter 11:
Guardian Heart—Part 1

YOU ARE THE CRAFTSMAN HARDEN, I PRESUME? I HAVE A REQUEST.

I WOULD LIKE YOU TO COME BACK TO WORK FOR ASTARIA.

......

TO PROTECT ASTARIA...

...I WANT YOU TO *FORGE* A *SWORD* LIKE THE *GUARDIAN HEARTS*!

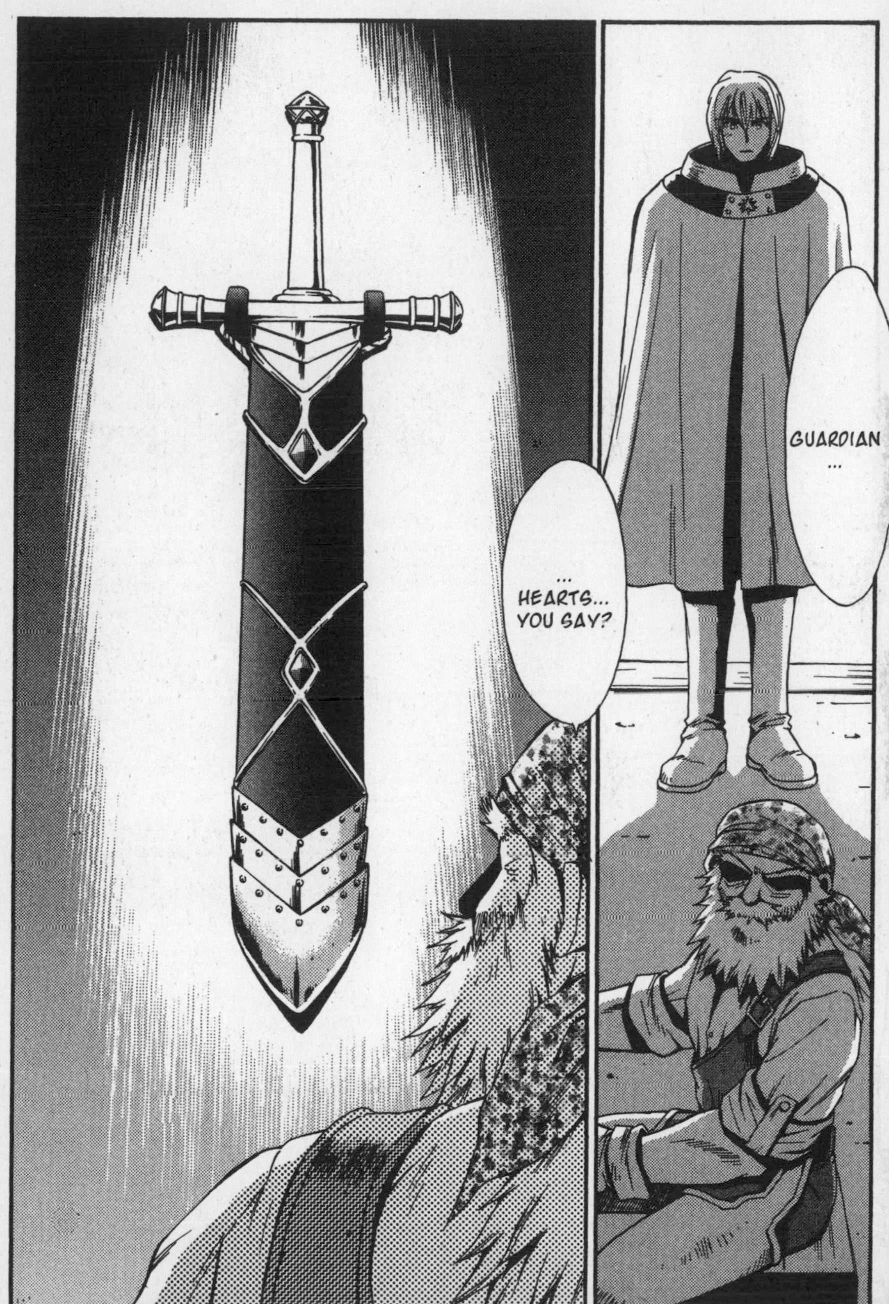
GUARDIAN
...
... HEARTS... YOU SAY?

I WANT AN IRON HATCHET OR AXE LIKE SENRI'S!

I CAN'T CUT WOOD WITH MY DULL OLD STONE KNIFE.

YOU'RE TOO YOUNG FOR SOMETHING LIKE THAT, COORO.

BESIDES, IRON-EDGED TOOLS ARE REALLY EXPENSIVE...

...MAINLY BECAUSE THE ASTARIAN GOVERNMENT CONTROLS THE IRON.

OOOH!
I WANT SOMETHING LIKE THAT!
NO! I TOLD YOU WE CAN'T AFFORD IT!
たたっ
HUSKY... WILL YOU BUY IT FOR ME?
I DON'T HAVE ANY MONEY.
UGH!
EARN IT YOURSELF!
I'M STARTING TO RUN OUT OF MONEY, TOO!
AT THIS RATE, WE'LL HAVE TO CAMP OUT EVERY NIGHT AND EAT NOTHING BUT FISH AND FRUITS!
NOOO! I DON'T WANNA!!
I WANT TO EAT BREAD! I WANT TO CHANGE CLOTHES!!
...?
THEN LET'S ALL WORK, THEN!
HERE, IN THIS TOWN!
OKAY?!

HUH?
OH, NO! WE DON'T HAVE ANY JOBS A KID COULD DO!

AND IF YOU'RE NOT FROM THIS TOWN, WE DON'T WANT YOU ANYWAY!
バタン
OOH!

WE CAN'T BLAME THEM FOR THINKING LIKE THAT.
IT'S NOT TRUE, THOUGH.
IF THEY KNEW WE WERE +ANIMA, THEY'D HAVE EVEN LESS WORK FOR US.

I THINK THERE ARE THINGS WE CAN DO **BECAUSE** WE'RE +ANIMA.
YOU KNOW, COORO, THAT'S NOT WHAT I MEANT...

ARE YOU LOOKING FOR WORK?

!

WHERE ARE YOUR PARENTS?

WE HAVE TO WORK BECAUSE WE DON'T HAVE ANY!

HUH?

COME WITH ME.

I'VE A NEED FOR HELPING HANDS...

CHILDREN'S HANDS... YOU KNOW?

WELL, I MIGHT HAVE SOME PHYSICAL LABOR FOR THE TALL BOY...

...BUT WHAT CAN THE LITTLE ONE DO?

UM... WELL...

くる
くる
くる

CATCH FISH...?

Ugh...

LEAP

くいっ
LOOKING CLOSELY, I SEE YOU HAVE A PRETTY FACE. ♡
WILL YOU BE A MAID AT MY BAR?

DON'T TEASE THE KID!
Come on!
Ha ha ha ha!
ピイッ
SENRI! LET'S KEEP GOING!!

Dang it!
What was she looking at?!
ムカムカ

?
SENRI?

!

ブルル…

......?
DOES IT FEEL LIKE WE'RE BEING WATCHED?
YEAH...
Gasp!

IT'S THAT...
...KIM-UN-KUR FROM BEFORE!!
IT'S THE ASTARIAN TROOP WE MET CROSSING THE MOUNTAINS!
THIS WON'T END WELL! SENRI, LET'S GO!
WHAT?! KIM-UN-KUR?!
COMMANDER!!
IT'S THAT HORRIBLE SOLDIER!
SENRI, HURRY!

!
WHA...!
WHAT ARE YOU DOING HERE?
ARE YOU FOLLOWING US?
OF COURSE NOT!
IN FACT, WE'D PREFER YOU WENT AWAY!

IT'S MORE UNUSUAL THAT A KIM-UN-KUR LIKE YOU WOULD BE IN ASTARIA!
LEAVE AT ONCE!!
......!

UWAAH!

BLOOD-THIRSTY BEAST! YOU SEE?! THAT'S THE TRUE NATURE OF A KIM-UN-KUR!
WE CAN'T LET HIM RUN LOOSE IN OUR LAND!
SENRI, STOP!!
OH MY...!
!
IS THAT...

...A
+ANIMA?!
SENRI!
AH?!
THE CROW
+ANIMA'S
HERE,
TOO!
OOWW!!
Ugh...!

......

HUSKY!!

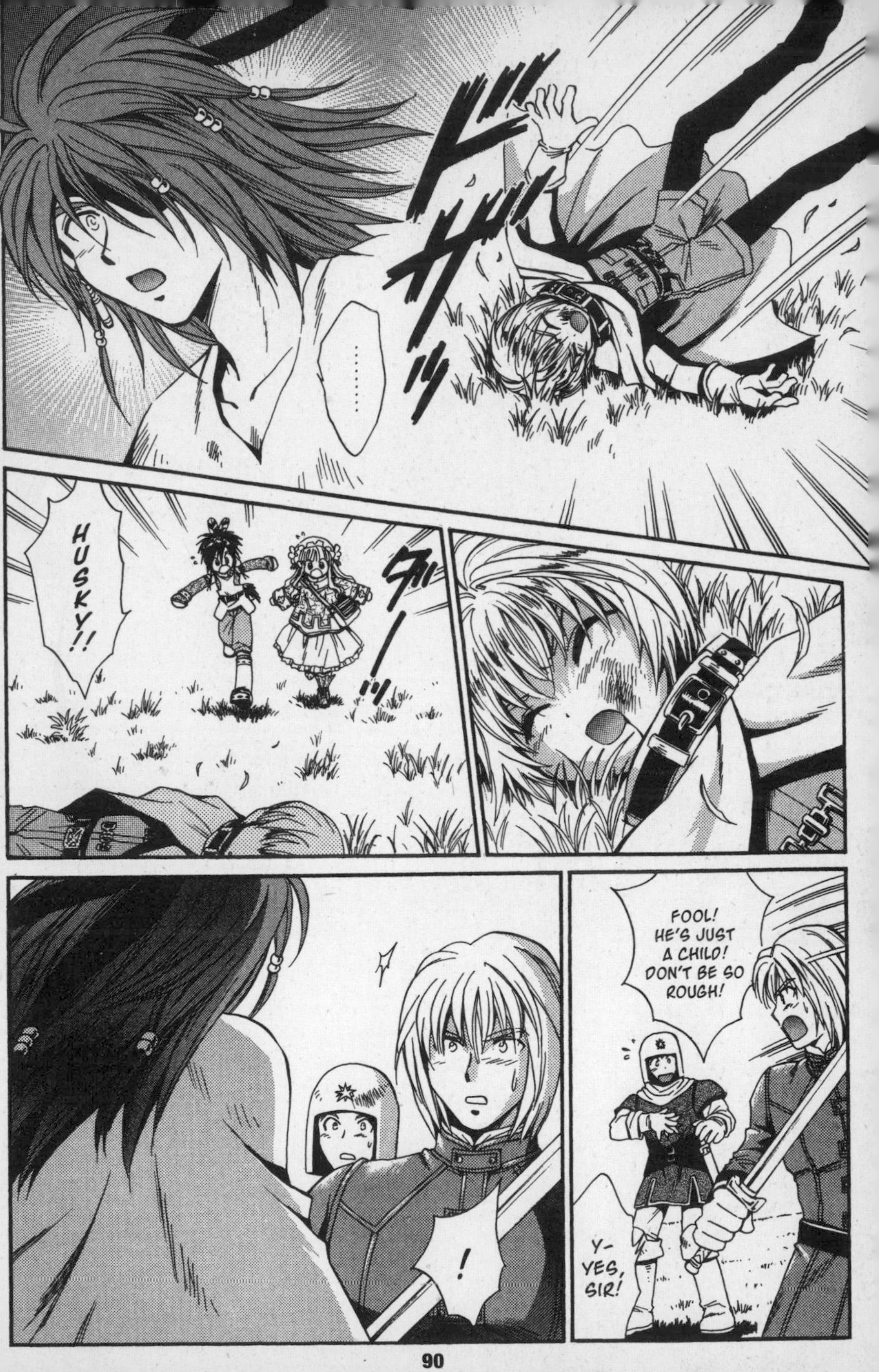

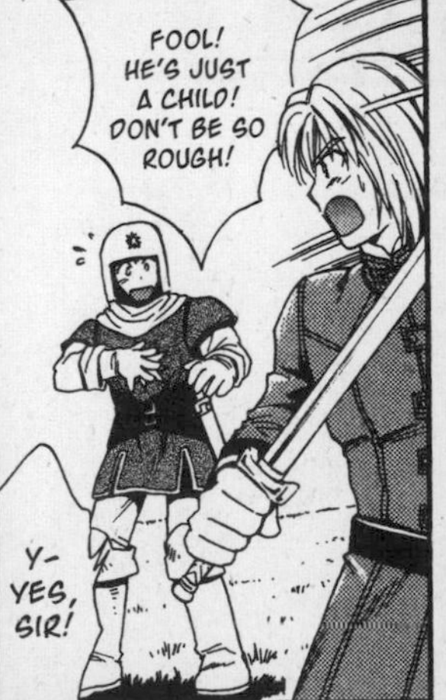

FOOL! HE'S JUST A CHILD! DON'T BE SO ROUGH!
Y-YES, SIR!

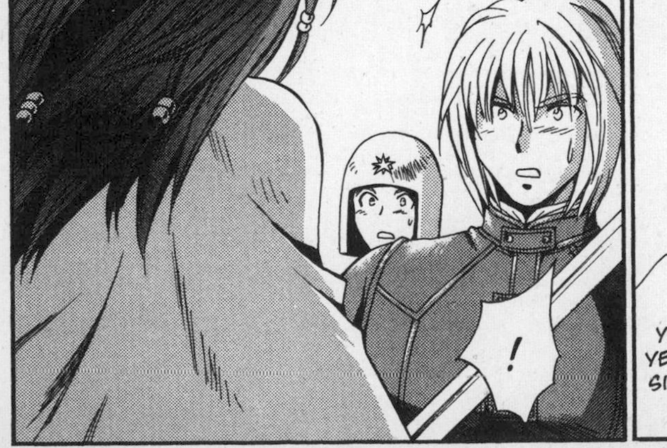

ゴゴゴゴ
HUSKY...
UH-OH...

EENNOOOOOUGH!!

H-
HARDEN!

MARGARET,
GO INSIDE.
HARDEN
...
YOU,
TOO.

AH!
ヒョイ

ぐい
SENRI! THIS WAY...!
ぐい

......
ギィ...
バタン

HARDEN ...
SO YOU TAKE THE SIDE OF +ANIMA...
ギリ

チョイ チョイ
......
YOU'RE HANDLING THIS WELL.
BUT IT'S OKAY TO TELL ME IF IT HURTS.
Okay, hold that there for a while.

THEY WERE THE ONES WE MET WHEN WE WERE CROSSING THE MOUNTAINS WITH ROSE AND MARGOT, RIGHT?
OOOH, REALLY! WHAT WAS WITH THEM?!

THEY CAME HERE SAYING THEY WANTED ME TO REFORGE THEIR SWORDS.

THEY EVEN BROUGHT A MOUNTAIN OF IRON SWORDS FOR ME TO WORK WITH.

EVEN THOUGH I'M...NOT A SWORD-SMITH ANY-MORE...

...I WON'T FORGE SWORDS FOR BATTLE AGAIN!

WHOA!!

THAT'S A BIG SWORD!!

WHAT IS IT...?

MY **HEART** IS FORGED INTO THIS SWORD...
IT WAS ABOUT TWENTY YEARS AGO...
BACK THEN I WAS BURNING WITH PATRIOTISM.
I KEPT FORGING SWORDS... JUSTIFYING IT BY SAYING IT WAS TO PROTECT THE COUNTRY.

くる

グイッ

SO YOU'RE ONE OF THE KIM-UN-KUR MOUNTAIN PEOPLE?
......
THE POWER OF A +ANIMA IS THE SAME AS A SWORD. THINK BEFORE YOU USE IT.
IT'S NOT SOMETHING YOU SHOULD USE TO RANDOMLY PICK FIGHTS.

ALL RIGHT!
THAT'S ENOUGH TALK! LET'S HAVE DINNER!
YUMMMM!! ♡♡

YOU CAN'T EAT SOLID FOODS, CAN YOU?
I WONDER IF YOU CAN HANDLE COLD SOUP?
THANK YOU...

UUMMMM!! ♡♡
YUMMY BREEEAD! ♡
EAT YOUR FILL SO YOU CAN HAVE ENERGY TO WORK!

WORK...?
YES!

I'M GOING TO MAKE THEM MY ASSIS-TANTS!
REALLY?

ばさっ

WE'RE GOING TO TAKE APART THESE OLD CLOTHES AND MAKE NEW ONES.

YAY! ♡

CHILDREN'S SMALL FINGERS ARE VERY USEFUL FOR THIS.

I'LL LEAVE YOU AT IT, THEN. GOOD LUCK--I'M COUNTING ON YOU!

We take this apart, right?

THEY'RE BOTH NICE, AREN'T THEY?

Take apart...

...

IT LOOKED LIKE THAT MAN UNDER-STANDS A LOT ABOUT +ANIMA.
MAYBE...

EH?
I DIDN'T SENSE A +ANIMA...
?
MAYBE THEY GET BETTER AT HIDING IT WHEN THEY'RE OLDER.
But I wouldn't know, anyway.

SO WHAT IF HE IS?
TO THINK WE'D END UP STAYING AT THE HOUSE OF AN OLD MAN WHO'S GOING AGAINST THE MILITARY!
THEY'LL THINK MORE AND MORE THAT WE'RE THEIR ENEMIES!

HE JUST DOESN'T WANT TO MAKE A SWORD.
THAT'S NOT BAD.
YOU THINK THAT'S A GOOD ENOUGH EXCUSE FOR THE MILITARY?!

THAT'S WHY IT'S EVEN MORE ANNOYING!
HE TALKS ALL HIGH AND MIGHTY!

OH YEAH...!

パッカーン

Meanwhile...

HEH HEH!
PHANTOM THIEF NANA LIVES AGAAAIN! ♡

Prank Girl !

Chapter 12:
Guardian Heart—Part 2

UUWAH ...
ごろん
バチッ
OW!!

Zzzz...
Snort!
COORO, YOU LITTLE--

HM?

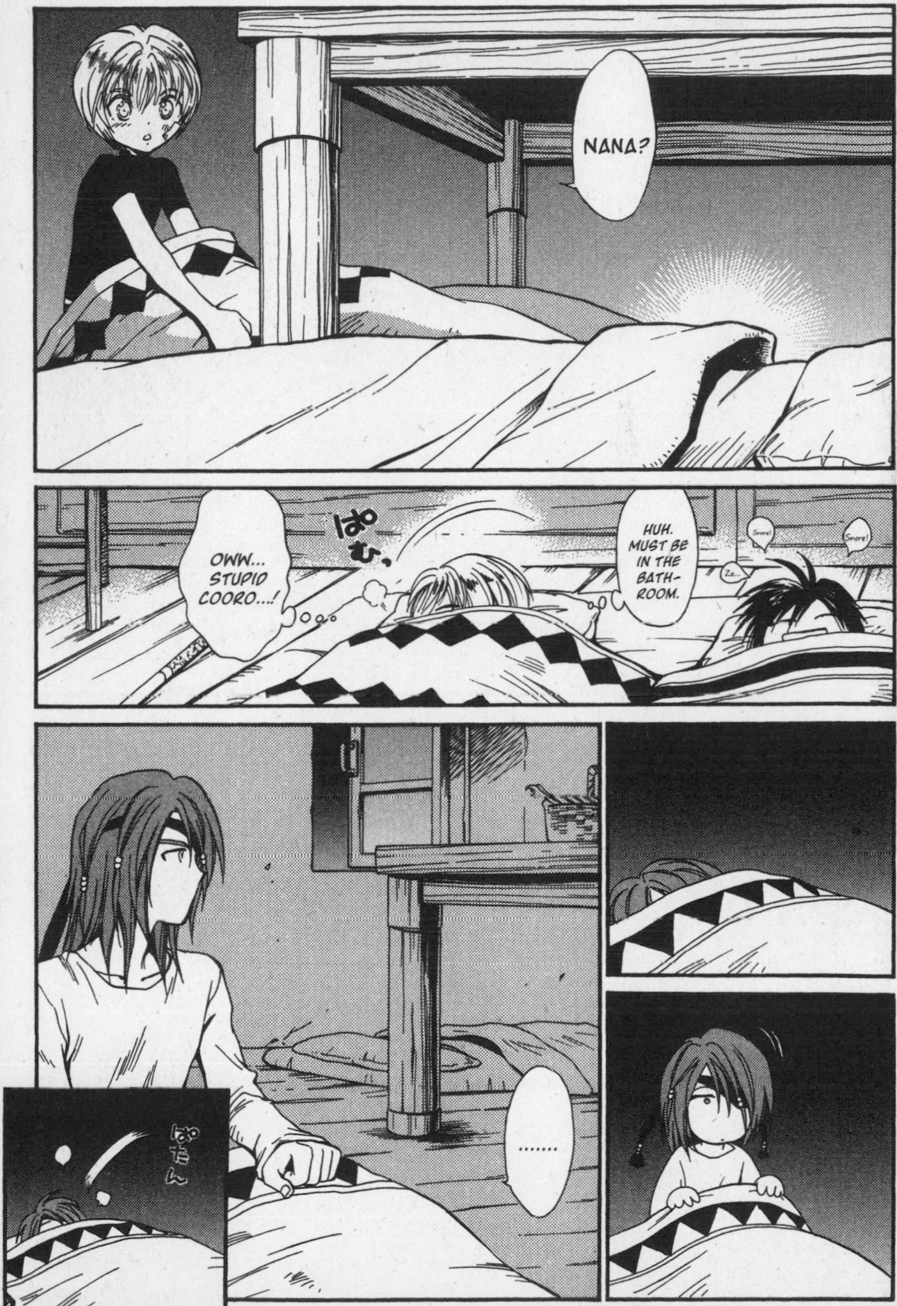

NANA?

Snore!
Snore!
Zz...
HUH. MUST BE IN THE BATH-ROOM.
ぱむ
OWW... STUPID COORO...!

....

ぱたん

THIS AFTER-NOON...
...WAS REALLY SOMETHING, WASN'T IT?

YEAH... THAT ONE +ANIMA WAS PRETTY SCARY.
AND HE WAS A KIM-UN-KUR, TOO...SO THE COMMANDER WAS EVEN MORE ANGRY...

EH? WHAT DO YOU MEAN?
YOU'RE A NEWBIE, SO YOU DON'T KNOW.
THE COMMAND-ER--

!

HEE HEE HEE! EXCELLENT!

YOU GO BEDDY-BYE WHILE PHANTOM THIEF NANA DOES HER JOB...

...MISTER SOLDIERS. ♡

GRAND-FATHER!
IGNEOUS ...
たた た
DON'T NEGLECT YOUR TRAINING.
YOU MUST PROTECT ASTARIA.
YES, SIR!

ガシャ
ガシャ
ガシャ
FLAP
!!
バッ
CLANG
!!

IF YOU FORCE HARDEN TO FORGE A SWORD FOR YOU, DO SO AT YOUR OWN PERIL...
A BLADE UNWILLINGLY FORGED IS DOOMED TO TURN **AGAINST YOU** IN YOUR **HOUR** OF **NEED!!**
WHAT IS THIS VOICE...
...ECHOING IN MY HEAD ...?!

......

KYAAAAH!!

OH NO... I MESSED UP!
I JUST NEED MY PLUNDER...
RE-TREEEAT!
UGH...!
ズルズル ズル
H-HEAVY...!
DON'T MOVE.
......

GOOD MORNING, HUSKY, SENRI!
MORNING.
WHERE'S NANA? IN THE BATHROOM AGAIN?
I JUST WENT, BUT I DIDN'T SEE HER.
OH...
GOOD MORNING!
WHERE'S NANA? IT'S TIME FOR BREAKFAST.

WHAT THE...?
LET HER OUT.
......
ばっ
THAT SACK...
DON'T TELL ME...
NANA!!
I knew it!

WHAT IS THE MEANING OF THIS?
THIS GIRL TRIED TO STEAL THIS AXE.
Grrrr!!
...
AN AXE...?
THIS BELONGS TO THE ASTARIAN GOVERNMENT.
I CAN'T LET HER GET AWAY WITH IT JUST BECAUSE SHE'S A CHILD.
A BAT +ANIMA... HMPH!
IF SHE DIDN'T HAVE +ANIMA POWERS, SHE PROBABLY WOULDN'T BE SO MISCHIEVOUS.
TOO MUCH POWER MAKES PEOPLE PROUD...AND BOLD...AND *FOOLISH.*

HARDEN ... DO YOU REMEMBER THE BATTLE OF MOSS MOUNTAIN?

YES. IT WAS A BATTLE WITH THE KIM-UN-KUR.

MY GRANDFATHER WAS KILLED BY A +ANIMA DURING THAT BATTLE.

MURDERED BY A *BEAR* +ANIMA, AS A MATTER OF FACT!

NOW, ASTARIA NEEDS YOUR STRENGTH AGAIN.
I WILL PARDON THE GIRL...
...AND IN EXCHANGE, I WOULD HAVE YOU FORGE ME A SWORD.

......

I MAY FORGE YOU A SWORD, BUT MY HEART WON'T BE IN IT.

IT WON'T BE A SWORD LIKE THE GUARDIAN HEARTS.

YOU HAVE THE HEART TO SAVE THIS GIRL, CORRECT?

IN THAT CASE, YOU SHOULD BE ABLE TO PUT HEART INTO THE SWORD AS WELL.

TAKE THE SWORD YOU BROUGHT WITH YOU TO MY FORGE.

BUT MISTER...!

FETCH THE SWORD!

YES SIR!

HEY, HEY, MISTER COMMANDER...?
WILL YOU LET ME HOLD THAT AXE?
EH?
とたたた

......
THANKS!

BOY...IT SURE IS HEAVY!
I CAN'T EVEN FLY WHILE HOLDING THIS.
HERE YOU GO...

IT'S IMPOSSIBLE FOR YOU, TOO, NANA.
It's too heavy.
MMPH MM-MM-MMMM!

NEXT TIME YOU WON'T FIND MERCY, GIRL.

......
Nyaaah
Nana, we're going.

STUPID!!

TRYING TO FRIGHTEN THE ASTARIAN MILITARY AWAY...
HOW BRAINLESS, NANA!
THAT WAS JUST WHILE I WAS THERE!
WHAT I REALLY WANTED TO DO WAS STEAL AN AXE FOR COORO!

AND *THAT'S* BRAINLESS, TOO!

WHY?!

NANA...

IT'S NOT GOOD TO STEAL.

I DO IT SOMETIMES, TOO...

...BUT WHEN I DO, I HAVE TO BE READY...

...SINCE I MIGHT GET BEATEN UP, OR EVEN KILLED.

IF YOU DON'T MIND THAT, WELL...

Y'KNOW WHAT I MEAN?

Y-YOU'RE RIGHT!

IF NANA HADN'T MESSED UP...
...MISTER HARDEN WOULDN'T HAVE TO REFORGE THAT SWORD.
SHEESH!

WHOA! THERE'RE SO MANY!
ARE YOU GOING TO REFORGE ALL OF THEM?

YES, I AM...
...THOUGH NO GOOD WILL COME OF IT.

THESE DAYS, I'M A SMITH WHO MAKES TOOLS FOR DAILY LIFE.
WHEN I MET MARGARET, I CHANGED...
MISS MAR-GARET?

DESIRING TO SEE MY SWORDS IN ACTION PROTECTING THE COUNTRY...
...I WENT TO THE BATTLEFIELD.
MANY OF THE GUARDIAN HEARTS I MADE WERE BRANDISHED THERE.
AMIDST THAT...
...I MET HER.

AS THE GUARDIAN HEARTS I FORGED WERE ABOUT TO HURT HER...
...MY ONLY THOUGHT WAS TO PROTECT HER!

MARGARET AND I STARTED A LIFE TOGETHER...
SOON, I STARTED TO ENJOY MAKING TOOLS FOR DAILY LIFE.
I STOPPED MAKING SWORDS...

...AND INSTEAD FORGED SCISSORS AND CARVING KNIVES.
AS RUSTY AND UNENTHUSED AS I AM NOW, ANY SWORD I MAKE IS SURE TO BE DULL.

HMMM...
IT'S A WASTE, ISN'T IT?
COME AGAIN?

YOU HAVE THIS MUCH IRON, AND IT'S GOING TO BECOME SWORDS THAT DON'T REALLY MATTER, RIGHT?

EVEN THOUGH THERE ARE SO MANY PEOPLE... WHO WANT CLEAVERS OR AXES.

HELP ME, SON. WE'VE GOT WORK TO DO!

THESE CHILDREN... THEY REALLY LIVE LIFE TO THE FULLEST, DON'T THEY?

THE POWER OF A +ANIMA IS THE SAME AS A SWORD. YOU USE IT TO PROTECT YOURSELF.

WHEN I STARTED LIVING WITH YOU, MY +ANIMA...
THAT IS BECAUSE YOU ARE MY GUARDIAN NOW.
...VANISHED.
...
Snore!
Snore!
Snore!

COMMANDER!
THE SWORDS ARE READY!
I'VE DONE ALL I CAN. TAKE THEM.
EXCELLENT!!

!
THIS... THIS ONE'S FULL OF CARVING KNIVES!
THIS BOX HAS SICKLES AND CLEAVERS...!
ブルブルブル

HARDEN!! JUST WHAT IS THE MEANING OF THIS?!

WHEN I PUT MY HEART INTO THEM, THIS IS WHAT THEY BECAME.

MY HANDS NATURALLY FORGED THEM.

Y'KNOW...

...THESE **ARE** VERY WELL MADE...

ほ——

I'D LOVE TO LET MY WIFE USE THIS...

WOULDN'T YOU?

WH-WHAT A MILITARY NEEDS ARE SWORDS...! NOT BLEEDIN' KITCHEN-WARE!
I DON'T CARE HOW WON-DERFUL THESE ARE!!
BUT COMMAND-ER...!
A MILITARY NEEDS TOOLS FOR DAILY LIFE, TOO!
IT WOULD BE SUCH A SHAME TO DESTROY THESE!!
GRRR...
......
ALL RIGHT ...!
WITH-DRAW!!
YES, SIR!

WHILE IT'S NOT SOMETHING ESSENTIAL FOR DAY-TO-DAY LIFE...

...IT CAN STILL COME IN HANDY.

A HATCHET!

IT LOOKS LIKE THOSE CHILDREN WILL STILL NEED THEIR +ANIMA POWERS FOR A WHILE...
Goodbye!
Thank you!
YES...
IT SURE DOES.

Chapter 13:
Husky's Melancholy
...

Astarian Capital—Astar
......
Ergh!

IGGY!
WAAAH!!
sigh
I'M IGNEOUS!
HOW SAD. I THOUGHT WE WERE CHILDHOOD FRIENDS...!
I THOUGHT I TOLD YOU TO STOP CALLING ME THAT!! I'M NOT A CHILD ANYMORE!!
FLY!
ANYWAY, I HEARD THAT YOU WERE COMING BACK FROM YOUR OFFICIAL TRIP.
SOMETHING ABOUT YOUR SWORDS BEING TRANSFORMED INTO SCISSORS AND KITCHEN KNIVES...?
snip snip
!

HOW DO YOU KNOW ABOUT THAT?!
IT'S SUPPOSED TO BE A **MILITARY SECRET!**
HAS IT LEAKED AS FAR AS THE RESEARCHERS?!
Oh!
WELL, YOU SEE... I'M SPECIAL. HEH HEH...
......
OH YEAH... I KEEP FORGETTING.
I JUST FILED A REPORT!
WELL, THERE GOES MY REPUTATION ...!
EVER SINCE I MET THOSE +ANIMA, THINGS KEEP GOING WRONG!
+ANIMA?

YES... A BLACK-WINGED CROW +ANIMA...
...A BAT +ANIMA...
...AND A KIM-UN-KUR BEAR +ANIMA.
THERE'S ONE MORE BOY, AND HE MIGHT BE A +ANIMA, TOO...
......
I UNDERSTAND THAT YOU HATE THE KIM-UN-KUR...
...BUT I DON'T KNOW ABOUT BEING SO HOSTILE TOWARD ALL +ANIMA...
BEFORE, +ANIMA MEANT KIM-UN-KUR! NOW THEY'RE BEING BORN IN ASTARIA, TOO!
IT'S PROOF THAT KIM-UN-KUR BLOOD COURSES THROUGH THEM ALL!
I CAN'T TOLERATE IT!

......
THAT'S NOT NECESSARILY TRUE...
WHAT?
MIGHT IT BE THAT A TIME HAS COME WHEN PEOPLE SHOULD ACCEPT +ANIMA POWERS?
YOU'RE SUCH AN OPTIMIST, FLY...
THAT'S RIGHT. SO YOU DO UNDERSTAND, IGGY!
I SAID STOP THAT!
THAT'S WHAT I THINK.
I JUST WISH I COULD HAVE ONE OF THOSE SWORDS THAT BECAME A KNIFE...
THEY'RE MILITARY PROPERTY, BUB!

A BLACK-WINGED +ANIMA...
IT MUST BE COORO.
SO HE'S MADE FRIENDS WITH A BAT AND A BEAR +ANIMA...
I WONDER WHAT TYPE OF +ANIMA HIS OTHER FRIEND IS...?

HUH? SENRI, WHAT ARE YOU LOOKING AT?
HARDEN... MARGARET...
OH!
THAT FLOWER WAS GROWING AT HARDEN'S HOUSE, WASN'T IT?
SO YOU PRESSED IT IN YOUR BOOK!
ANYWAY... NANA SURE IS LATE.
I MEAN, HOW LONG DOES A CRUMMY BATH TAKE?!
I DON'T THINK SHE'S BEEN GONE THAT LONG...
OF COURSE NOT!!
??

SORRY I TOOK SO LONG!
ぴょんっ
TADAH!!
WHAT DO YOU THINK?
くるくる
......
AH! YOUR CLOTHES!
NANA, HOW DID YOU GET THEM?
I HAD MARGARET MAKE THEM. AREN'T THEY NICE?
SIGH... SEE? THIS IS WHY I HATE GIRLS!
THEY FUSS OVER THINGS LIKE THAT, AND MAKE PEOPLE WAIT FOREVER WHILE THEY TAKE A BATH!
ぐ...
......

HUSKY, YOU WERE FUSSING OVER CLOTHES, TOO!
YOU THINK I CAN STAND WEARING LEAVES?!
LEAVES ...?

カー
ッ
WHAT DO YOU MEAN?

C-COORO, SENRI!
GO TAKE A BATH!
NO PROBLEM!
LET'S GO, SENRI!

Taking a bath...♪
Taking a bath...♪

YOU'RE NOT GOING, HUSKY?
ゴロン
NOPE.

HUSKY NEVER TAKES A BATH.
IT'S NOT LIKE HE'S SMELLY OR DIRTY, SO IT'S OKAY, BUT...
...EVEN THOUGH I'M A GIRL, HIS FACE IS WHITER AND SMOOTHER...
...AND PRETTIER...
Gasp!
MAYBE, JUST MAYBE...
...HUSKY...
...IS A GIRL?!

WE'VE COME PRETTY FAR SOUTH.

ARE WE AT THE OCEAN YET?

IT LOOKS LIKE WE STILL HAVE A LONG WAY TO GO.

AS LONG AS IT'S WARM, WE DON'T HAVE TO GO THAT FAR, DO WE?

IT REALLY WOULDN'T BE CRAZY TO SAY HE'S A GIRL...!
THE REASON HE NEVER TAKES A BATH WITH ANYONE...
...IS THAT HE SECRETLY BATHES AT NIGHT SO KNOW ONE WILL FIND OUT HE'S A GIRL!
SOUNDS RIGHT!
HEY, THERE ARE A BUNCH OF OPEN SHOPS OVER THERE!
LET'S GO TAKE A LOOK!
LET'S MEET BACK HERE LATER.
SOME-TIMES I JUST WANT TIME BY MYSELF...
!
WHEN THE SUN HAS MADE IT TO THAT TOWER... WE'LL MEET RIGHT HERE, OKAY?
OKAY!
YEAH. SURE.
......

HE STARES AT JEWELRY LIKE HE'S IN A TRANCE...
A BOY WOULDN'T BE INTERESTED IN THAT, WOULD HE?
WHAT DO YOU THINK OF THESE PENDANTS, MISS? ♡
SEE?!

HUSKY! YOU...

...HAVE A BIG **SECRET**, DON'T YOU?

THA-THUMP
AH-HA!
BINGO!!
......

......
A SECRET...? EVERYBODY HAS SECRETS.

YEAH...
R-RIGHT...!
B-BUT...

...I'M A GIRL, SO...
...IF THERE'S SOMETHING YOU CAN'T SAY TO COORO OR SENRI, JUST KNOW YOU CAN TALK TO ME ABOUT IT!
OKAY?!
WHAAAA?!

WH-WHY WOULD I TALK TO A GIRL ABOUT ANYTHING?!
AH! HUSKY!
OOOH! ♡
THAT COLOR WOULD LOOK GOOD ON YOU, HUSKY!
WHY DON'T YOU GROW YOUR HAIR OUT, TOO, HUSKY?
I THINK IT WOULD BE PRETTY! ♡
......

......
NANA...
YES?
DO I LOOK THAT MUCH LIKE A GIRL?
PLEASE... DON'T MAKE FUN OF ME.
HUSKY...!
I REALLY...
...HATE WOMEN!!
NANA, IS SOMETHING WRONG?
AH...

I THINK MAYBE HUSKY SAYS HE HATES GIRLS...
...TO HIDE THE FACT THAT **HE'S A GIRL!**
HOLY--?!
HUSKY'S A GIRL?!

COME TO THINK OF IT...
...HUSKY WAS REALLY PRETTY AS THE LITTLE MERMAID PRINCESS.
M-MERMAID PRIN-CESS?

BUT... HUSKY SAID HIMSELF THAT HE'S A BOY.
SEE? IT'S WEIRD THAT HE'D POINT IT OUT!
RIGHT, SENRI?!
...??
THEN WE'LL JUST HAVE TO *FORCE IT OUT OF HIM...!*
NANA?

......
IT'S TRUE...
HUSKY IS SO MUCH LIKE A GIRL...
HIS SKIN IS SO WHITE, AND HE'S SO SLENDER...
LOOKING LIKE THAT, HE'S VERY...
snicker...

AH, IT'S HUSKY...!
Heh heh!
YOU'RE NOT WEARING A SKIRT TODAY?
Ha ha ha!
IT'S SO WEIRD FOR A GIRL TO WEAR BOY'S CLOTHES...
ブチッ!!
I AM NOT A GIRL!!!

I...
...HATE GIRLS...
HEY ...!
YOU!
WHAT ARE YOU DOING? NOTHING?
EH?
I HAVEN'T SEEN YOU AROUND HERE.
WANT TO COME WITH US? COME ON, DO YOU?

ISN'T THAT ONE A LITTLE YOUNG TO PLAY WITH US?

THAT'S WHAT I LIKE! ♡ AND SHE'S PRETTY TO BOOT!

SO THAT'S YOUR TYPE, HUH...?

YEAH. RIGHT, SWEET-HEART? ♡

......

HUSKY'S LATE...

YEAH...

IS IT BECAUSE I WAS SO NOSY...?

BUT...

Waaah!! Kyaaah!!

FIGHT! FIGHT!

HUSKY!!
Waaaaaahh!!
Waaaaaahh!!
YEOWCH!!
YOU BRAT!
DON'T GET A SWELLED HEAD JUST BECAUSE YOU'RE A LITTLE CUTE!!
......
GYAAAAAHH!
S-SENRI, NO!!
IT'S MORE IMPORTANT TO GET HUSKY OUT OF THERE!!
ALL RIGHT!

HEEEEY!!
Wha?
UP HERE, UP HERE!
OH!!
+ANIMA?!
Ah!

IT'S OKAY, SENRI. PUT ME DOWN.

......
バサ
バサ
バサ
ARE YOU OKAY, HUSKY?

HUSKY...

REMEM-
BER
WHEN...
...I TOLD YOU
ABOUT WHEN
I BECAME A
+ANIMA...?
THAT WAS MY
NUMBER ONE
SECRET.
BUT AS
MUCH AS
I WANTED
TO KEEP IT
SECRET...
...I
THOUGHT IT
WOULD FEEL
THAT MUCH
BETTER IF
I TALKED
ABOUT IT.
THAT'S
WHY...

THAT'S WHY...
HERE GOES!! ♡
HUH?!
...

......
SEE? I TOLD YOU!
WHAT...?
YEAH, IT LOOKS PRETTY.
WHAT DOES...?
はっ

HUH...?!
WHAT HAVE YOU...?!
ARGHH!!
ぱっ
ホーーッ
AT LEAST THEY LEFT MY CLOTHES ON...
WHY AM I WEARING THIS DRESS?!!
COORO!
HMM?
SO IT COULD BE EASIER ON YOU, HUSKY...
TAKE YOUR CLOTHES OFF!!
HEY!!

I'M A BOY!! B-O-Y!!
Husky...
Wow, that was fast!
WHY AM I STANDING HERE?
'CUZ I'D LOOK BAD IF IT WAS JUST ME!
......
ぬぎー
GYAAAAH!!
IS... IS IT TRUE?
HUSKY, YOU'RE REALLY...
...A BOY?
YES, IT'S TRUE!
THAT'S NOT A SECRET-- IT'S NOT ANYTHING!

BUT HUSKY... YOU WON'T TAKE A BATH WITH COORO AND SENRI...
HUH?
YOU FORGET...

...I GO IN THE WATER ALMOST EVERY DAY TO GET FISH!!
OH...
OOHHH!!

"OOHHH" MY BUTT!!
WHY HIT ME?!
AND YOU, SENRI! JUST STOP IT!
HEY...YOU WERE A "MERMAID PRINCESS" ...?
......

He is clever at mimicking.

モワァー
シュワ〜
WHAT IS THIS PLACE?
THERE'S STEAM EVERY-WHERE.
AND DOESN'T IT SMELL WEIRD TO YOU?
HUH?
ホカ ホカ
EGGS...?

Chapter 14:
Scars

YOUBOSO

SO IT'S THE HOT SPRINGS TOWN, BUBBLY?

HOT SPRINGS?

POOLS FILLED WITH HOT WATER.

IT'S GOOD FOR YOUR BODY TO BATHE IN THEM.

WOW! I WANT TO TRY THAT!

ME, TOO!

AH...!

ON...ON SECOND THOUGHT, I DON'T WANT TO...

BUT WHY, NANA? IT SOUNDS LIKE FUN...!

It's not scary, right?
Probably not...
HNH?
WELL, WELL...
IF IT ISN'T SENRI!
LOOK!
NANA, COORO, HUSKY!
IT'S ROSE!

Heh heh! ♡
MAINLY BECAUSE THEY'RE FEELING GOOD AFTER BEING IN THE HOT SPRINGS.
IN A TOWN LIKE THIS, TOURISTS ARE MORE LIKELY TO SPEND FREELY.
THAT'S RIGHT!
YOU'RE PEDDLING IN THIS TOWN?
NO, NOT YET.
HAVE YOU BEEN IN A HOT SPRING, ROSE?
EMPTY, HE SAYS! THAT SOUNDS GOOD. WANNA GO?
ER...
THERE'S AN EMPTY HOT SPRING OVER THERE.
AND THERE'S AN INN... A REAL GOOD ONE!
UH... UMM...

IN THAT CASE, OKAY!
LET'S GO TO THE HOT SPRING!

WELCOME!

IS THIS YOUR INN?
THERE REALLY ISN'T ANYONE HERE.
'CAUSE IT'S SO FAR ON THE EDGE OF TOWN, I GUESS...

Y-YOU'LL BE STAYING HERE, RIGHT?
THAT WILL BE AN ADVANCE PAYMENT OF TEN GILLAH PER PERSON, PER NIGHT.
THAT'S CHEAP.
THAT'S BECAUSE IT'S SO RUN-DOWN.
YEAH... BUT OUR HOT SPRING HAS THE BEST "BEAUTY WATER" IN TOWN!
THAT'S RIGHT!
BEAUTY WATER...?!
キラーン
THE BOYS' BATH IS THAT WAY.
THE GIRLS' BATH IS THIS WAY.
YOU'RE COMING IN TOO, RIGHT HUSKY? EVEN THOUGH IT'S NOT COLD WATER.
YES, I'M GOING IN.
THEN, WE'LL GO THIS WAY.
NO PEEPING!
WHO'D WANT TO?!
ムカー
Looking at girls... ick!

YAAAAAY!!
ざっぱーん
HOT HOT HOT HOT HOT!!!
OH YEAH--BE MINDFUL OF THE HOT SPOTS.
THE WATER HERE IS LUKEWARM.
YOU BE CAREFUL, TOO, SENRI...

チャポ…

THAT'S SOME SCAR...

ARE THEY CLAW MARKS...?

Oohh!

YOU HAVEN'T SEEN THEM 'CAUSE YOU'VE NEVER TAKEN A BATH WITH US, HUSKY.

WAIT!

SENRI, IT'S HOT OVER THERE!

チャプ チャプ

GREAT! I RELAX FOR A S-SECOND, AND...!
Shut up, shut up!
バシャバシャ
HYAAHH!
...
THE BOYS SURE ARE LIVELY.
SOUNDS FUN!
Uwaah!!
ROSE'S...
...+ANIMA MARKINGS...
Aah...
OH...
A SCAR...!

WHAT ...?
THIS...?
LET'S JUST SAY YOU CAN GET INTO MANY DANGEROUS SITUATIONS WHEN YOU'RE A +ANIMA.

BUT...
...I'M NOT UNHAPPY THAT I BECAME A +ANIMA.
MAINLY BECAUSE I'M THE ONLY ONE WHO CAN PROTECT MY LITTLE BROTHER.

MY...
...+ANIMA MARKINGS STAND OUT...
...SO I THOUGHT I SHOULDN'T GO TO A HOT SPRING.

I TRY NOT TO SHOW THAT I'M A +ANIMA, EITHER.
IF I KEEP IT THAT WAY, THEN THINGS ARE SETTLED WITHOUT PEOPLE WORRYING MORE THAN THEY HAVE TO.

PFFT! TELL THAT TO COORO AND SENRI!
THEY'LL BOTH TRANSFORM AT THE DROP OF A HAT!
REALLY?
I WONDER IF THEY'D UNDER-STAND...

......

ISN'T IT NICE THAT WE HAVE CUSTOMERS TODAY?

IT IS THE FIRST MONEY WE'VE SEEN IN A LONG TIME.

IT SEEMS LIKE THOSE CHILDREN HAVEN'T HEARD THE RUMORS ABOUT US.

AS LONG AS IT DOESN'T SHOW UP...

ちゃぷ…
ROSE'S SKIN WAS SO PRETTY.
EVEN WITH HER SCAR...IS THAT WHAT THEY CALL AN ADULT GLOW?
I HAVE TO SCRUB MYSELF TWICE AS HARD!
オー
Become smoother and smoother!
Smooth, smooth!
SPLISH

SPLISH ...?
もわ…
EEEEEK!!

EH?!
NO! DID IT APPEAR...?!
YAAAAAAAHHHH!!
"IT"?
はっ
PLEEEASE!!
ガバァー
WHOA!
I'M BEGGING YOU!! DON'T LET THIS GET OUT!!
UH... THAT IS...
IT STARTED APPEARING IN THE MIDDLE OF THE NIGHT ABOUT HALF A MONTH AGO...
GYAAH!
THE FRIGHTENED GUESTS SPREAD RUMORS ALL THROUGH TOWN.
IT RUINED OUR BUSINESS, WHICH IS WHY OUR INN WAS SO DESERTED TONIGHT...

WE JUST RAN OUT OF MONEY...! WE'RE SO HUNGRY...!
IF ANY MORE RUMORS GET STARTED--
IT'S NOT JUST A RUMOR!!

I SAW IT!
IT WAS ALL HAIRY!
AND AS BIG AS A SMALL MOUNTAIN!
A BEAR?
...
NO...

IT'S A +ANIMA.

HMM... IN THAT CASE, WE HAVE NO CHOICE BUT TO HIRE SOMEONE AND GO ON A MOUNTAIN HUNT OR SOMETHING...!
WE DON'T HAVE ANY MONEY, BUT THERE'S NOTHING ELSE TO DO.
WHAT?!
W-WAIT...! YOU CAN'T!
Um, that is...
......
HEY...
SHOULD WE TRY CHASING IT AWAY?
COORO?!
REALLY?!
CAN YOU--WOULD YOU--DO THAT?!
Grr!
...
IF WE CAN, WILL YOU GIVE US BACK THE MONEY WE PAID YOU?
M-MONEY?
G-GIVE BACK...?
WELL, ALL RIGHT...
10 x 5 = 50 gillah...

BUT IT'S A +ANIMA LIKE US! WE CAN'T CHASE IT AWAY!
SHUT UP, NANA.
OH, COORO, WHAT ARE YOU THINKING?!
AND YOU, TOO, ROSE, SENRI!
HOW CAN YOU BE OKAY WITH THIS?!
LET'S JUST SAY YOU CAN GET INTO MANY DANGEROUS SITUATIONS WHEN YOU'RE A +ANIMA.
OH...
IF HE GETS CAUGHT IN A MOUNTAIN HUNT... HE WON'T GET OFF EASILY...
...BECAUSE HE'S A +ANIMA.
AT LEAST THIS WAY WE COULD TRY TALKING TO HIM AND HAVE HIM LEAVE WITHOUT RESORTING TO VIOLENCE.
I SEE...
WHAT WAS I THINKING?
NOT TO MENTION WE CAN GET BACK THE MONEY WE PAID! ♡
These boys...

I WONDER WHAT KIND OF +ANIMA HE IS.
MAYBE HE REALLY IS A BEAR?
I wonder...
FUR?
......
BISON...
A COW...?

STOMP
STOMP

ザブ
AAAAHH...

!!

AH!
WAIT, SENRI!
WHA...?
WHAT ARE YOU DOING?!!

WAH!!
WARGH!!
YOU'RE PLANNING TO CHASE ME OFF, AREN'T YOU?
WELL IT AIN'T GONNA HAPPEN!
I HAVE A RIGHT TO USE THE HOT SPRING, TOO!!

M-MISTER! CALM DOWN!
WE--
SHUT UP!!
KYAAHH!
OOP!

WHAT'S THIS?!
A +ANIMA...?
!!

MORON! LET GO, DARN IT!!
IT'S HOT HERE!!
HEY!!
....
SENRI ...
HOT HOT HOT HOT HOT!!
HOT HOT HOT HOT HOT!!

HAA...
HAA...
HUFF...
ARE YOU OKAY, MISTER?

......
HUH...?

WHAT? YOU'RE ALL JUST KIDS!
AND... YOU'RE +ANIMA...?
YUP! THAT'S RIGHT!

HUH?
OH! MISTER...
...THAT LOOKS PAIN-FUL!

OH, THIS?

IT HAPPENED WHEN I WAS IN +ANIMA FORM.

WOUNDS HEAL EASIER IN THE FORM YOU WERE IN WHEN YOU GOT THEM.

THE HOT SPRING HERE WORKED REALLY WELL.

SO DID THE OWNER OF THIS PLACE ASK YOU TO STAND GUARD HERE?

UM...

HE WAS SAYING THEY'D START A MOUNTAIN HUNT FOR YOU!

MISTER, YOU GOTTA RUN AWAY!

MY WOUND... HAS FINISHED HEALING.
I DON'T NEED THE HOT SPRING ANYMORE.
I'LL GO.
YOU ALL...
...STAY HEALTHY.

THE +ANIMA LEFT?!
THANK GOODNESS!!
Yaaay!
WELL THEN, HERE'S YOUR MONEY, AS PROMISED!
It can't be helped. I did promise...
HUH?
GIVE US MORE.
IF YOU ONLY PAID US BACK WHAT WE GAVE YOU, IT WOULDN'T HAVE BEEN WORTH THE TROUBLE.

W-WAIT, COORO!
YOU CAN'T--
MISTER BISON LEFT FOR US.
WE HAVE TO DO AT LEAST THIS MUCH!

AH...

IT WAS AWFUL...
SEE? I GOT SCRAPED HERE!
MAYBE WE'LL TELL EVERYONE THAT THERE'S A MONSTER STILL...
OKAY, OKAY!
PLEASE DON'T!!!

THERE ARE ALL KINDS OF +ANIMA...
...WHO LIVE WITH THEIR OWN SCARS.
OUR +ANIMA POWERS LET US LIVE...
...BUT THEY SOMETIMES HURT US EVEN MORE.

To be continued...

Favorite Foods
Cooro's favorite food is apples! It's a common, simple red fruit, and its round shape invites a feeling of fullness--so it fits Cooro perfectly. Apple pie, baked apples, bread covered in apple jam, and of course raw apples! Well...Cooro will eat anything, except he doesn't like bitter things because he's a little kid.
Apple pie.♡ He likes it jam-packed with filling.
Dried fish
Husky makes me wonder if he has a favorite food. I get the feeling that he doesn't care whether food tastes good. He'd probably say, "When I'm hungry, it doesn't matter what I eat, as long as I get some nourishment." If I had to pick something, I'd guess he'd like clean, fresh food. He wouldn't like greasy or sweet foods as much, and he prefers fish to red meat. That makes me think, "Isn't that like cannibalism?" (teasing Husky)

Senri's favorite food is...honey.
It's not really because he's a bear +Anima
(maybe that's half of it...). Honey is a mountain
treat, sweet and full of nourishment. I don't get
the feeling that Senri would gobble food down;
he seems like he'd eat slow. I get the feeling
that he'd savor anything edible, little by little.
Senri seems like he'd like sweet things, so he
might like sugar candy.
A piece of
honeycomb
Nana is fairly domestic. She can easily
do needlework and cook. She was raised
doing housework, so of course she became
good at it. She's had no experience with
fancy foods. Her favorite food is fresh-
baked bread. She can't bake it when
camping, so to her, bread is the symbol
of a safe home. She also seems to like
vegetable soup and the like.

TOKYOPOP

COORO AND THE GANG STUMBLE UPON A TOWN WHERE CITIZENS ARE ENTERTAINED BY NON-LETHAL GLADIATORIAL MATCHES. COORO WANTS IN ON THE ACTION...BUT DOES THIS HUMBLE HERO HAVE WHAT IT TAKES TO BE A BURLY BRAWLER? UNBEKNOWNST TO OUR HEROES, FIGHTING IS THE LEAST OF THEIR WORRIES IN THIS CRUEL COLISEUM, AS THE GAMES HOLD A DARK SECRET THAT THREATENS TO BRING THEIR TRAVELS TO AN ABRUPT END!

THE CLAWS COME OUT IN THE NEXT BONE-BRUISING VOLUME!

4

Natsumi Mukai

WARCRAFT
THE SUNWELL TRILOGY

TOKYOPOP®

RICHARD A. KNAAK · KIM JAE-HWAN

From the artist of the best-selling *King of Hell* series!

It's an epic quest to save the entire High Elven Kingdom from the forces of the Undead Scourge! Set in the mystical world of Azeroth, *Warcraft: The Sunwell Trilogy* chronicles the adventures of Kalec, a blue dragon who has taken human form to escape deadly forces, and Anveena, a beautiful young maiden with a mysterious power.

www.TOKYOPOP.com/warcraft

www.TOKYOPOP.com

SPOTLIGHT TOKYOPOP MANGA SUPPLEMENT

THE DREAMING

BY QUEENIE CHAN

ALL OF THEM VANISHED...WITHOUT A TRACE.

When twin sisters Amber and Jeanie enroll in an Australian boarding school, they soon uncover a dark, unexplained secret: Students have been known to walk off into the surrounding bushlands, where they have vanished completely! Few know how the girls disappeared...fewer yet know why. Amber and Jeanie soon realize that the key to unlocking a secret that has been hidden for years may lie in the world of their dreams!

SUSPENSE-HORROR SHOJO FROM THE CREATOR OF THE HIT WEB COMIC *BLOCK 6*.

FOR MORE INFORMATION VISIT: WWW.TOKYOPOP.COM/THEDREAMING

STOP!

This is the back of the book.
You wouldn't want to spoil a great ending!

This book is printed "manga-style," in the authentic Japanese right-to-left format. Since none of the artwork has been flipped or altered, readers get to experience the story just as the creator intended. You've been asking for it, so TOKYOPOP® delivered: authentic, hot-off-the-press, and far more fun!

DIRECTIONS

If this is your first time reading manga-style, here's a quick guide to help you understand how it works.

It's easy... just start in the top right panel and follow the numbers. Have fun, and look for more 100% authentic manga from TOKYOPOP®!